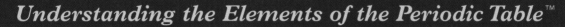

Understanding the Elements of the Periodic Table™

OXYGEN

Michele Thomas

8   16

O

rosen central™

The Rosen Publishing Group, Inc., New York

For my mom, Vivian, a breath of fresh air

Published in 2005 by The Rosen Publishing Group, Inc.
29 East 21st Street, New York, NY 10010

First Edition

Library of Congress Cataloging-in-Publication

Thomas, Michele, 1978–
Oxygen / Michele Thomas.—1st ed.
    p. cm.—(Understanding the elements of the periodic table)
Includes bibliographical references and index.
Contents: What is oxygen?—Oxygen and the periodic table—Oxygen and our world—Oxygen and combustion—Oxygen compounds—Oxygen and life—The periodic table.
ISBN 1-4042-0159-9 (library binding.)
1. Oxygen—Juvenile literature. [1. Oxygen. 2. Periodic law—Tables.]
I. Title. II. Series.

QD181.O1T52 2005
546'.721—dc22

2003027998

On the cover: Oxygen's square on the periodic table of elements. Inset: The subatomic makeup of the oxygen atom.

Manufactured in the United States of America

Contents

Introduction

On August 20 and again on September 9, 1975, scientists at the National Aeronautics and Space Administration (NASA) launched two unmanned spacecraft named *Viking 1* and *Viking 2* into outer space. Their mission was to search for signs of life on Mars. After a ten-month journey, the two spacecraft entered into orbit around Mars and released landers that touched down on July 20 and September 3, 1976.

Viking 1 landed at the Chryse Planitia, a rolling, boulder-strewn plain with scattered dusty dunes and outcrops of bedrock. These rocks are believed to be worn-away remnants of volcanic rock from billions of years ago. *Viking 2* landed at the Utopia Planitia, a similar volcanic plain nearly 4,000 miles (6,500 kilometers) away, with shallow troughs that may have been caused by sheets of ice expanding and receding across the Martian surface. Both of these landers transmitted hundreds of measurements and color photographs back to Earth. Several of their scientific experiments were designed to discover whether there were bacteria living in the soil and to find evidence of oxygen, an essential element for life.

While the missions provided many clues about Martian history and taught us that Mars is more like Earth than any other planet in our solar system, scientists never did find what they were looking for—solid evidence that life exists or once existed on Mars.

This photo, taken by a Mars exploration rover in 2004, shows the lifeless landscape of the Red Planet. For decades, scientists have been debating the existence of oxygen on Mars. So far, their research has turned up traces of water, a substance largely composed of oxygen. NASA is developing a device with which astronauts can produce their own oxygen on Mars.

However, scientists were not discouraged. In early 2004, NASA landed a spacecraft on the Martian surface. This time, the craft returned information giving evidence that water once existed on Mars. Water contains large amounts of oxygen, so life may have existed on Mars.

It is the presence of oxygen here on Earth that gives our planet life. This single element allows us to breathe, gives plants the ability to grow, and helps keep our planet warm. The element oxygen, which you cannot see, feel, or taste, sustains all life on Earth. Oxygen is an important element, one that we cannot live without—literally!

Chapter One
What Is Oxygen?

Take a deep breath. Now, take another. Can you smell the oxygen in the air? Probably not. That's because oxygen is an odorless, tasteless, and colorless element. Elements are made of only one kind of substance, known as an atom. These elements are the building blocks of matter. Try thinking about matter as a giant puzzle that creates everything in the universe. Elements are the puzzle pieces. By fitting the pieces together in one way, you can create a grain of sand. Try different combinations, and you can create a drop of water, a rock, or even a person!

It is not enough to say that oxygen is important to life on Earth. You may not be able to see, taste, or touch oxygen, but it is very real and absolutely essential to life in our world. Without it, our planet might look more like Mars or the Moon—dry and lifeless. There would be no clouds, rain, or snow because they each require water, which is nearly 90 percent oxygen by mass. (Hydrogen accounts for the remaining 10 percent.) There would be none of the beautiful plants and animals that you see every day because oxygen is vital to nearly every organism on Earth.

There are more than 100 elements that scientists have discovered so far. As old as Earth is (a healthy 4.5 billion years old), many of the elements have been identified only during the past few hundred years. Oxygen was "officially" discovered by two chemists working independently during the eighteenth century: Karl Scheele of Sweden and Joseph Priestley of England.

In 1773, Scheele discovered oxygen while experimenting with nitric acid, a colorless liquid that can cause severe burns and is often used in fertilizer. When he heated nitric acid, a gas was released that made nearby candles burn brighter. Scheele wrote that the atmosphere is composed of two gases. One supports combustion, or burning, which he called "fire air." The other, which he called "foul air," prevents combustion.

A year or so later in England, Priestley discovered that the gas

English chemist Joseph Priestley is credited with being the first person to identify oxygen as an element. Although his experiments came more than a year after Scheele's, Priestley was the first to publish his findings. Antoine Lavoisier would take Priestley's findings one step further by developing theories on combustion, or why things burn.

released by heating a mixture of mercury (Hg) and air also made candles burn brighter. He published his findings in 1775, two years before Scheele, and took most of the credit for the discovery of what he called "dephlogisticated air." It was another scientist, Antoine Lavoisier, who, as we'll see later, would give oxygen its name and realize that it was an essential chemical element.

Oxygen and Our Puzzling Universe

Before we go any further, let's talk a little more about these "puzzle pieces" and how they fit together to create everything in our universe. For starters,

Karl Scheele

Born on December 9, 1742, Karl Scheele was a well-respected chemist by the time he was thirty years old. Although he did not receive primary credit for discovering oxygen, his record as a discoverer of other substances is probably still without equal. Scheele isolated and investigated many chemical compounds, including citric acid, which is found in fruits such as oranges, grapefruits, lemons, and limes. His study of manganese dioxide in 1774 led him to discover another element, chlorine, and barium oxide—a mixture of the elements barium and oxygen. Scheele also invented many techniques for studying chemical elements and reactions. He was also the first to prove that the same metal may go through different stages as it develops rust.

Although he was elected to Sweden's Stockholm Royal Academy of Sciences in 1777, Scheele preferred his work as an apothecary (pharmacist) to that of a university professor. In the last years of his life, he was the first to isolate arsenic acid (1775), molybdic acid (1778), lactic acid (1780), tungstic acid (1781), and prussic (or hydrocyanic) acid (1783). Remarkably, he made most of his discoveries in spite of his poverty and lack of proper laboratory equipment.

each element, or puzzle piece, is made up of atoms, which are the smallest pieces of an element that still have that element's properties. An atom is one specific element, such as an atom of carbon (C) or an atom of oxygen (O). Two or more atoms together make a molecule. Join one atom of carbon with with atom of oxygen you get a molecule of carbon monoxide (CO).

Subatomic Particles

Atoms themselves are made up of smaller parts called subatomic particles, which include protons, electrons, and neutrons. Protons have a positive electric charge, electrons have a negative electric charge, and neutrons have no charge at all. If you were to view an atom through a very powerful microscope, you would find it is largely made up of empty space.

The nucleus, or center, of an atom contains the protons and neutrons. The nucleus is pretty small and heavy compared to the rest of the atom. An element's atomic number is equal to the number of protons contained within its nucleus. Since an oxygen atom contains eight protons, its atomic number is 8. Another important property of an element is its atomic weight (or atomic mass). The atomic weight is the average sum of the number of protons and neutrons in each atom of the element. Electrons are very light and do not really factor in to the weight. Oxygen has an atomic weight of 15.9994.

Outside of the nucleus are shells that contain the electrons. The first shell of an atom can hold only two electrons, the second shell can hold up to eight, and the third shell can hold up to eighteen. The oxygen atom has only two shells of electrons. The inner shell

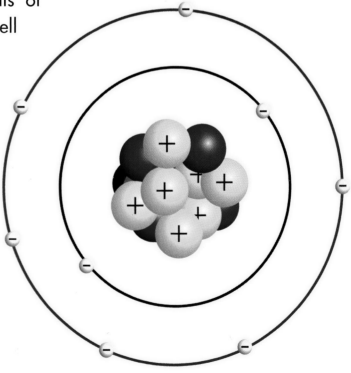

All atoms are made up of subatomic particles, including protons, neutrons, and electrons. One atom of oxygen contains eight protons and eight neutrons in its nucleus. Eight electrons orbit the nucleus in two shells, or layers. These electron shells allow oxygen to bond, or combine, with other elements.

Oxygen Isotopes

An atom of oxygen has an equal number of protons and neutrons in its nucleus, unless it's an isotope. An isotope is an atom that has the same atomic number but a different number of neutrons and protons. For example, oxygen-17, an isotope of normal oxygen, contains eight protons and nine neutrons. Oxygen-18 has ten neutrons. Because they have no electrical charge, the presence of extra neutrons usually has little effect on the properties of the element. However, they can change the atomic weight.

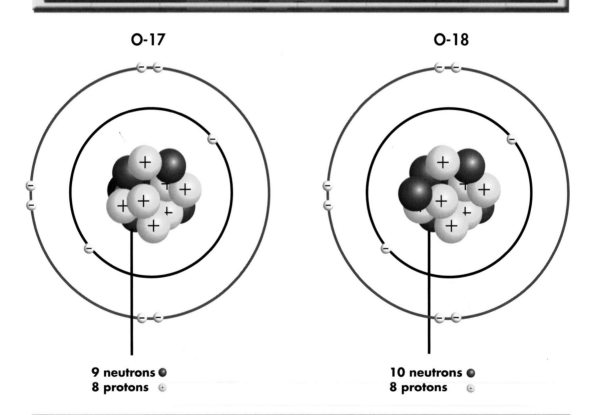

O-17

O-18

9 neutrons ●
8 protons ⊕

10 neutrons ●
8 protons ⊕

Oxygen has two heavy isotopes, oxygen-17 and oxygen-18. Every element on the periodic table has one or more isotopes. The word "isotope" comes from ancient Greek, with *iso-* meaning "equal" and *topos* meaning "place." Therefore, an isotope of an element will be located in the same place on the periodic table as the element, regardless of the isotope's differing atomic weight.

Oxygen 8 O 16 Snapshot

Chemical Symbol:	O
Properties:	Nonmetal; odorless, colorless, tasteless
Discovered By:	Independently by Joseph Priestley and Karl Scheele
Atomic Number:	8
Atomic Weight:	15.9994
Protons:	8
Electrons:	8
Neutrons:	8
Phase at Room Temperature:	Gas
Density @ 293 K:	1.429 kg/m^3
Liquid Phase:	-297°F; -183°C; 91 K
Solid Phase:	-360°F; -218°C; 55 K
Commonly Found:	Everywhere

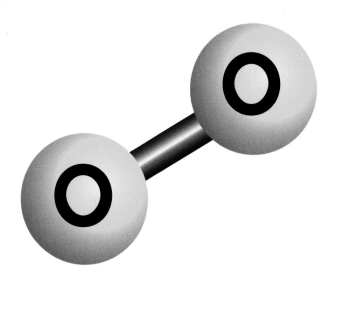

Oxygen, in its gaseous form, is most commonly found as a diatomic molecule (O_2). This is when two oxygen atoms bond together with a covalent bond. As a diatomic molecule, the two oxygen atoms are stable. Oxygen can also be found in two unstable forms, O (one oxygen atom) and O_3 (three oxygen atoms).

contains two electrons. The outer shell contains six electrons. The behavior of an atom is strongly influenced by the electron distribution in its shells.

So, how does this electron distribution impact the behavior of an oxygen atom? An atom is the most stable when its electron shells are completely full (with two electrons in the first shell, eight in the second, and so forth). Knowing that oxygen has an atomic number of 8, we also know that it has eight protons and eight electrons. With only six electrons in its outer shell, oxygen is always on the lookout for two more electrons to complete its outer electron shell to stabilize the atom. This means that oxygen is highly reactive. In fact, most oxygen atoms in the air are combined in pairs called diatomic molecules, a name that means having two atoms. This is why oxygen almost always appears as O_2. When oxygen combines with two hydrogen (H) molecules, it forms perhaps Earth's most important compound, water (H_2O).

Each Atom Is Unique

It is the combination of subatomic particles that makes oxygen unique among the other elements on the periodic table. If we were somehow able to take away a proton from oxygen, leaving it with seven protons, it would be a totally different element—nitrogen (N). If we were able to add a proton, making it nine protons, it would become another element—fluorine (F). So the number of protons in the nucleus of an atom determines what element it is.

The makeup of oxygen's protons, neutrons, and electrons gives it the ability to bond, or join, very easily with other elements to form compounds. This is one of the reasons why oxygen and oxygen compounds are so common in our universe and why oxygen is one of the most important elements on the periodic table.

Chapter Two
Oxygen and the Periodic Table

With so many elements to keep track of, scientists began to look for ways to organize them. In 1869, Dmitry Mendeleyev, a Russian chemist and professor at the University of St. Petersburg, created a special table to help his students remember the elements. He placed the elements in horizontal rows, or periods, according to their atomic weight. The lightest element was placed at the left and the heaviest at the right. Little did he know that his simple idea would help revolutionize the way scientists understood chemistry. The table allowed scientists to really see for the first time the relationships, trends, and patterns among elements. These relationships and trends are called properties. Properties are the characteristics of an element, such as color, taste, smell, and chemical behavior.

While the table was not widely accepted at first, with time, scientists realized that it was a pretty good idea. In fact, the modern periodic table is very similar to Mendeleyev's original design. Today, the periodic table still uses Mendeleyev's arrangement of periods, in which elements are placed on the periodic table according to their atomic number. The elements are also organized into groups. The number of the group appears above each column of the table. In the same way that members of the same family often resemble one another, elements within these groups have similar chemical properties. In fact, these groups are often referred to as "families" of elements. By arranging the elements this way, scientists could predict whether any given element was a metal, a nonmetal, or a metalloid, which is an element that has the properties of both a metal and a nonmetal.

Two New Elements

The periodic table was designed to allow for the addition of newly discovered elements. Since Mendeleyev first designed the table, more than fifty elements have been added. Even in the twenty-first century,

Dmitry Mendeleyev's periodic table of elements changed science forever. Above is one page of Mendeleyev's table as it was published in 1869. Mendeleyev's design left gaps in the table to allow for elements to be discovered.

elements are still being added. In January 2004, a team of Russian and American scientists announced the creation of two elements. These new elements would fill in gaps at the lower end of the table. Element 113 is named ununtrium (Uut); element 115 is named ununpentium (Uup). But they're not written in stone yet. The existence of Uut and Uup have to be verified by other scientists before they are given a permanent place on the periodic table.

Oxygen on the Table

Oxygen is located within group VIA on the periodic table, which also contains sulfur (S), selenium (Se), tellurium (Te), and polonium (Po). As

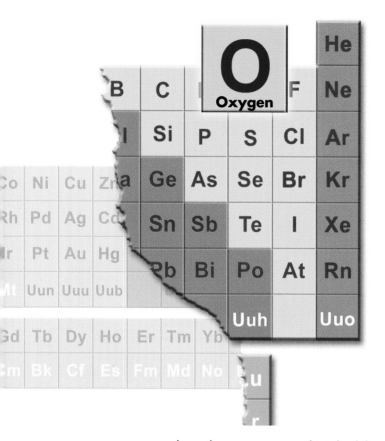

Oxygen is located in group VIA (or 16) on the periodic table. All elements in group VIA have six electrons in their outermost shell. This means that each element in group VIA has room for two more electrons in its outer shell and will bond easily with others. The staircase line separates metals from nonmetals on the table. Elements that border the line are known as metalloids and have properties of both metals and nonmetals. Most of the elements to the right of the staircase line are gases.

you can see, the elements are divided by a staircase line that extends from boron (B) to astatine (At) in the lower right portion of the periodic table. This staircase line separates the metals from the nonmetals. Metals like potassium (K), sodium (Na), and iron (Fe) are located to the left of this line. Nonmetals, such as chlorine (Cl) and nitrogen are located to the right of the line. Oxygen is located on the right side of the staircase line with the other nonmetals.

The Properties of Oxygen

Properties are the characteristics of an element. One such property is the physical state of an element at room temperature. All elements can appear in one of three physical states, called phases: solid, liquid, or gas. At room temperature, oxygen is a gas. When cooled to a temperature of

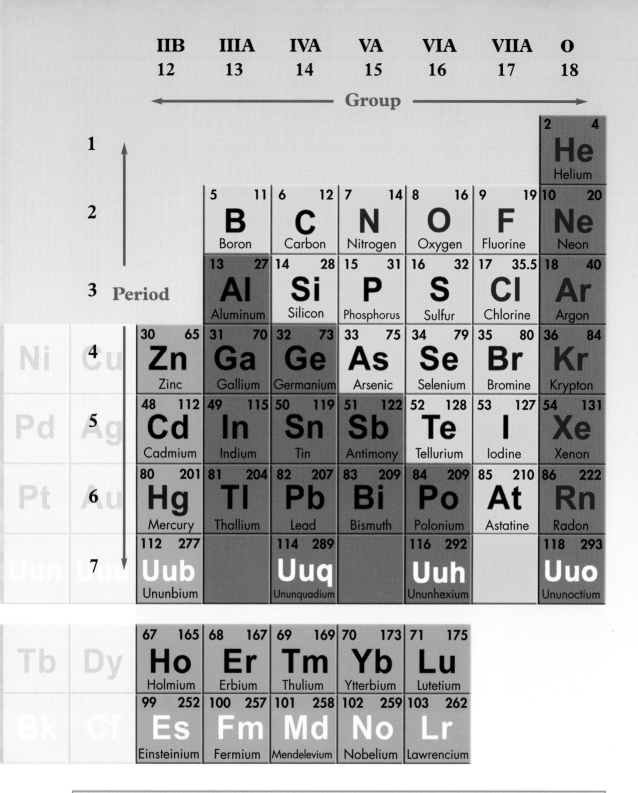

On the periodic table, elements are arranged from left to right by increasing atomic number. This indicates the number of protons in an atom's nucleus. There are seven periods on the periodic table. The bottom two rows, which include holmium (Ho) and einsteinium (Es), are the lanthanide and actinide series of elements. These are also known as the rare earth elements because they are rarely found as pure elements.

Liquid Oxygen in Space Travel

Did you know that liquid oxygen is essential to space travel? Liquid fuel rockets have two tanks—one containing liquid oxygen and the other containing liquid hydrogen. When the two are mixed and ignited in the rocket's main combustion chamber, they cause a hugely powerful controlled explosion. This helps propel the spacecraft beyond the powerful pull of Earth's gravity. The fuel burns to produce an exhaust of water vapor.

Liquid oxygen is used as a fuel to propel spacecraft. Jets use oxygen in Earth's atmosphere to provide fuel for combustion to propel the plane. But spacecraft must make their own fuel for combustion while in outer space.

-360°F (-218°C)—far below anything that occurs naturally on Earth—oxygen becomes a solid. Oxygen's boiling point is higher than other elements in the air. This allows oxygen to be extracted from the air by a cooling process that involves alternately compressing and expanding air in pressure-sealed containers. When the air temperature cools to nearly -279°F (-183°C), it becomes a liquid. Oxygen can then be distilled and stored as a liquid in pressurized metal containers.

Chapter Three
Oxygen and Our World

You might say that elements are the substances that make the universe tick. And oxygen is the element that makes Earth tick. Oxygen is the most abundant element on Earth, and it takes up the most space. Oxygen makes up nearly half of our planet's bulk, or mass. Every 100 pounds (45 kilograms) of Earth's crust contains about 47 pounds (21 kg) of oxygen.

Based on observations of the Moon and the planets in our solar system, the weather would also be pretty rough in an oxygen-free world. The atmosphere—the mass of air that surrounds Earth like a blanket—would be much thinner, for starters. Scientists believe that with far less atmosphere to protect Earth's surface from solar radiation and no clouds to help trap the Sun's warmth, Earth's weather might more closely resemble that on Mars: windy, with fierce dust storms, and really, really cold. Imagine a world where the average temperature on a sunny day is about -10°F (-23°C). Without oxygen, Earth wouldn't be a nice place to live at all. Who would have imagined that something so tiny and simple could be so important?

The Elixir of Life

Oxygen wasn't always so important. In fact, until just a few billion years ago, there wasn't much oxygen on this planet at all. Scientists believe that Earth started out as little more than a big rock surrounded by a cloud of gases that would be harmful to people, plants, and animal life. These gases included methane (CH_4), hydrogen, and ammonia (H_3N). A combination of substances in the rock and increasing pressure very slowly built up enough heat to melt the interior of the planet. The heavier materials, such as iron, sank toward the middle of this "Earth soup," while lighter silicates, or rocks made of silicon (Si) and oxygen, rose to the surface to form Earth's earliest crust.

Oxygen and the Atmosphere

There are many theories about how Earth's atmosphere became rich with oxygen. According to one theory, the heating of Earth's interior caused other chemicals inside the planet to rise to the surface and be released into the air. Some of these chemicals formed water (H_2O), while others combined to form the gases of the atmosphere. Over millions of years, the water slowly collected in low places of the crust and formed the oceans. It is believed that oxygen first appeared in large amounts within the atmosphere nearly 3 billion years ago, when cyanobacteria, or blue-green algae, first appeared and began producing energy through the process of photosynthesis.

During photosynthesis, green plants and some bacteria use energy from the Sun to combine carbon dioxide (CO_2) and water to make food. The light used in photosynthesis is absorbed by a green pigment, called chlorophyll, within each food-making cell. The sunlight causes water to split into molecules of hydrogen and oxygen. In a series of complicated steps, the hydrogen combines with carbon dioxide from the air, forming a simple sugar. Oxygen from the water molecules is given off in the process. It most likely took quite some time—millions of years—to build up enough oxygen in the atmosphere to support larger and more complex forms of life on Earth, including people.

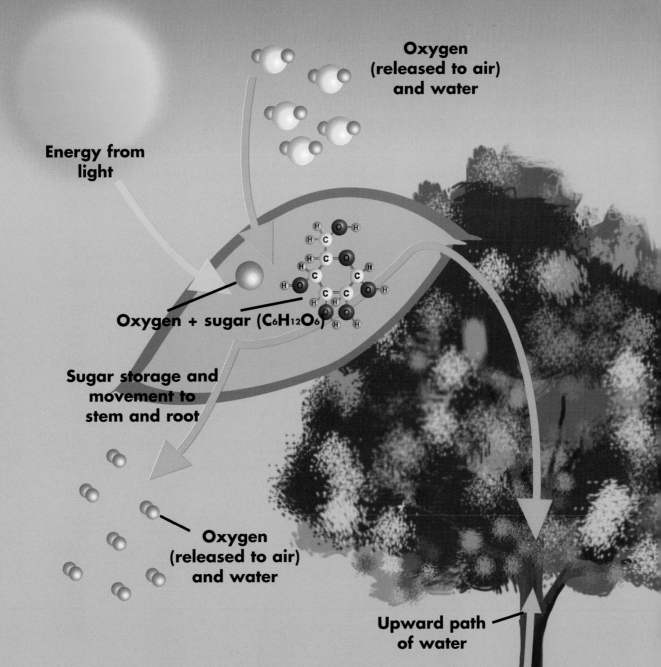

Oxygen
(released to air)
and water

Energy from
light

Oxygen + sugar ($C_6H_{12}O_6$)

Sugar storage and
movement to
stem and root

Oxygen
(released to air)
and water

Upward path
of water

Photosynthesis is one of the most
important processes for sustaining life
on Earth. Without it, our atmosphere
would run out of oxygen. During
photosynthesis, plants absorb
energy from the Sun and turn it
into chemical energy. This energy is
then used to absorb carbon dioxide—
which is exhaled by animals—and
convert it into oxygen.

Water (from soil)

Even before people knew what oxygen was, they knew it was important to life. Throughout history, especially before the eighteenth century and the discovery of oxygen, many people thought that the air was made up of only one substance. As you will see, the study of oxygen is closely linked to the study of the air. In fact, it is not uncommon for people to use the two words interchangeably today, even though they are quite different.

The air is more accurately called the atmosphere, and it covers the land and sea and everything in between. It covers our whole planet and extends far above its surface. The air is invisible and has no taste or smell. Yet, it is as real as anything you can see, taste, or touch. This atmosphere—the air that we breathe—is actually a finely tuned mixture of gases. Oxygen makes up about 21 percent of that mixture. The remaining 79 percent of the air is a combination of several other gaseous elements.

Nitrogen 78%

Oxygen 21%

Other 1%

Earth's atmosphere supports and protects all life on the planet. Without it, we wouldn't be able to breathe, and we would be burned up by the Sun's intense heat. The atmosphere is primarily composed of nitrogen (78 percent, in red) and oxygen (21 percent, in blue). Several other gases compose the remaining 1 percent of the atmosphere.

Oxygen and the Ozone Layer

A molecule that is made up of three oxygen atoms (O_3) is called ozone. Ozone can exist in the upper layers of the atmosphere, where it helps protect Earth against harmful ultraviolet (UV) rays from the Sun. However, close to the ground, ozone is the main component of smog and can cause serious damage to your lungs. Ground-level ozone is a product of reactions involving chemicals called hydrocarbons and nitrogen oxides in the presence of sunlight.

Scientists are concerned because many forms of air pollution have been proven to damage the ozone layer. Without the ozone layer protecting us, the Sun's rays can greatly damage plants and the eyes and skin of animals, including people. This intense sunlight may also

The Air Up There

Here is a closer look at the special ingredients that make up our atmosphere.

Gas	Percentage by Volume
Nitrogen	78.084
Oxygen	20.946
Argon	0.934
Neon	0.0018
Helium	0.000524
Methane	0.0002
Krypton	0.000114
Hydrogen	0.00005
Nitrous oxide	0.00005
Xenon	0.0000087

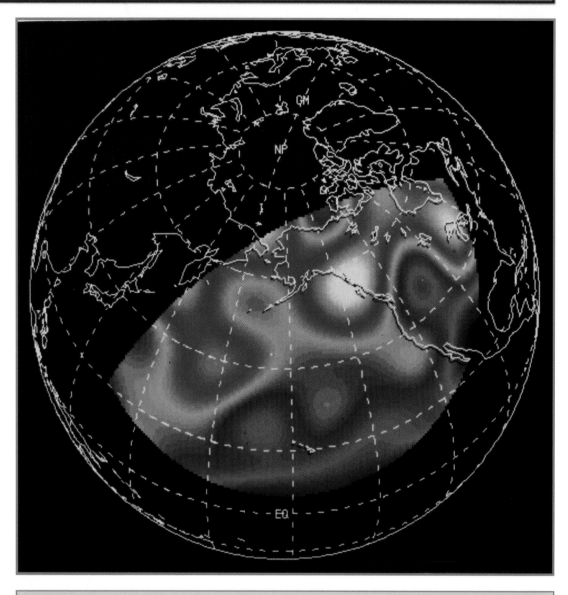

Ozone exists in Earth's upper atmosphere and helps protect us from harmful cosmic rays. However, pollution is creating a hole in the atmosphere's ozone layer. This orthographic, or layered, image shows damage to the Earth's ozone layer. The red and white areas depict the most damage.

lead to the melting of Earth's polar ice caps, causing the level of the oceans to rise and, over time, wear away the land on which we live.

Chapter Four
Oxygen and Combustion

One of oxygen's most important, yet destructive, roles in our world is combustion, or burning. When something burns, it reacts with oxygen to create light, heat, and energy in the form of fire. In order for anything to burn, oxygen must be present.

Millions of years ago, people were both frightened and fascinated by the warmth, beauty, and power of fire. It provides essential warmth and light, as well as the means to prepare food. It's also very dangerous. After all, just one spark could lead to a fire that can destroy everything in its path. In the thousands of years man has known about combustion, we have made little progress in controlling fire.

Fire is not a solid or a liquid. To ancient cultures, fire seemed more like the wind, except that it was hot and bright and could do just about whatever it wanted. No wonder ancient people believed fire was magical! Many cultures from the Far East to India, Iran, Greece, and North and South America even worshiped fire. Even cultures that didn't worship fire thought it was essential to life.

The History of Combustion

Some of the earliest efforts to understand air and fire date back many thousands of years to the philosophers and physicians of the ancient

Fire was one of the earliest things for humans to discover. For millions of years, fire has been the key to survival for humankind. Without oxygen, fire would not exist. Oxygen feeds fire, and combustion occurs only in the presence of oxygen.

world. As early as 545 BC, Anaximenes, a Greek philosopher, argued that the world developed out of air. He believed that air turned into other things, like water and earth, through a process called rarefaction. This process might be thought of as similar to condensation, the process by which a gas turns into a liquid. According to Anaximenes, air becomes visible through rarefaction, first as a mist or cloud, then as water, and finally as solid matter like rocks. If the air is further rarefied, it turns to fire.

Around 450 BC, Empedocles, another Greek philosopher, came to believe that air must be one of the basic elements from which all matter is created. At the time, people believed the elements were earth, fire, and water. A poet, statesman, and physician, Empedocles also believed that nothing in the universe could be created or destroyed—material could only be transformed into other objects depending on different combinations of the four essential ingredients. As we've already seen, this early scientist may have been wrong about some of the details, but he was definitely on the right track.

In the eighth century, a Chinese alchemist named Mao-Khóa is said to have believed that the atmosphere is composed of two invisible

Combustion is a rapid chemical reaction that usually produces heat and energy in the form of flame. Combustion occurs when a substance reacts violently with oxygen during the process of oxidation. Oxidation can be so rapid and intense that combustion can cause explosion or detonation.

components called yin and yang. According to Mao-Khóa, yin was "incomplete air" that bonded easily with many substances. By heating charcoal or saltpetre, a substance often used in gunpowder, yin is removed from the air. Mao-Khóa believed that yang was "complete air." While there is no evidence today of his experiments, Mao-Khóa was almost certainly on a journey of discovery that European scientists would complete hundreds of years later, when they realized that air wasn't a single element at all but a mixture of gases. Mao-Khóa's yin and yang would eventually became known as oxygen and nitrogen.

One of the first people to catch on to the idea that the air was actually a mixture of gases is perhaps more famous for his artistic contributions than his scientific ones. "Where flame cannot live, no animal that draws breath can live," wrote Leonardo da Vinci, the legendary Italian painter and sculptor who lived during the late fifteenth century. He observed that a fire needs to use a part of the air around it in order to burn. During his study of the human body, da Vinci discovered that the same relationship plays a role in the process of respiration, or breathing. He watched the air being taken into the body with every breath as a candle burned nearby. He concluded that it was impossible for air to be an element because it was obviously composed of different parts. Finally, a breath of fresh air!

Phlogiston: The Wrong Road

By the start of the eighteenth century, scientists had different ideas about air and fire. They had figured out that the universe was made of more than water, air, fire, and earth. A German chemist and physician named Georg Ernst Stahl came to believe that anything that could burn was in part composed of a substance called phlogiston. Fire, he reasoned, was caused by the release of this substance into the air. Stahl called his theory phlogiston theory. The word "phlogiston" comes from Greek and means "burned." The ash or residue was called "dephlogisticated." The phlogiston theory was widely accepted in the 1700s and led to many findings in chemistry.

The major objection to this theory was that the ash of an organic substance, such as wood, often weighed less than the original substance. Meanwhile, calx, or metallic ash, was heavier than the metal. One of the scientists who studied these weight differences was a French chemist named Antoine Lavoisier. During his own experiments with fire, he realized that Scheele's "fire air" helped the calx gain weight by chemically combining with some of the air around it and not by absorbing phlogiston. Later, he noticed that this same "fire air" tended to form acids when mixed with certain substances. From the Greek words *oxys*, meaning "acid," and *genos*, meaning "forming,"

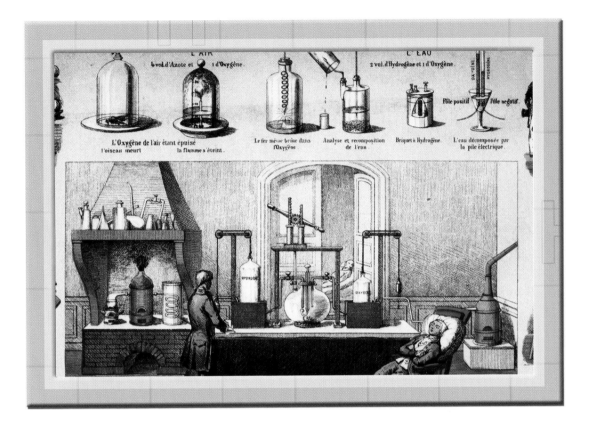

This engraving shows scientists in 1790 using Lavoisier's apparatus to perform the recomposition of water. This experiment showed that water was formed by the combustion of hydrogen in oxygen. This reaction occurred in a ratio of two hydrogen atoms to every one oxygen atom. Therefore, scientists were able to conclude that the makeup of water was H_2O.

Lavoisier renamed the gas oxygen. A number of chemists—including Joseph Priestley, one of the discoverers of oxygen—rejected Lavoisier's findings, however, and tried to retain some form of the phlogiston theory. By 1800, practically every chemist recognized the correctness of Lavoisier's oxygen theory.

Combustion and Our World

Today, combustion helps generate electricity in power plants, and it provides the power for car and train engines, airplanes, and even

The Father of Modern Chemistry

Born in Paris in 1743, Antoine Lavoisier is often called the father of modern chemistry. In 1766, at the age of twenty-three, he was elected to the French Royal Academy of Sciences after writing an essay on how fuel burned in street-lamps. He discovered not only that air is made of nitrogen and oxygen but also that water is made of hydrogen and oxygen. Lavoisier was also the first scientist to arrange chemicals into family groups and explain how some chemicals formed new substances when mixed. His research between 1770 and 1790 helped to discredit the phlogiston theory. Having also served as a leading tax official and public administrator before the French Revolution, Lavoisier was executed with other financiers during the revolutionary terror.

spacecraft like those used to send astronauts into outer space. Scientists define combustion as an exothermic reaction—a chemical reaction that creates heat and light. This reaction is a form of oxidation between a gas and a fuel source. A fuel can be anything that burns, like wood or charcoal. The gas is oxygen from the air, although other gases, like chlorine, may also be involved.

Fire is a chemical process. Three things are needed for this process: oxygen, heat, and fuel. Without one of these elements, a fire cannot start or continue. During this chemical process, the molecules within oxygen and the fuel rearrange themselves. Energy is either released or absorbed. The process in a fire is called oxidation, in which oxygen atoms combine with hydrogen and carbon to form water vapor and carbon dioxide.

Fuels burn only when they have been heated to a certain point, called the ignition temperature. The heat, usually from a match or

Without exception, fire cannot exist without oxygen. In this experiment, a glass container is filled with pure oxygen. A wooden stick is lit, then blown out. While the burnt section is still red-hot, it is dipped into the container of oxygen (*photo 1*). In the presence of oxygen, the burnt stick immediately reignites (*photo 2*). When the stick is pulled from the container, the flame dies (*photo 3*) because there is not enough oxygen in the air to provide fuel to keep it burning.

Fighting Fires

The job of a firefighter is to control and put out fires. The best way to do this is by limiting the supply of oxygen in a burning area. Firefighters do this by soaking the area with water, spraying foam from fire extinguishers, or using specially made blankets that do not burn—anything to cut off the supply of air to the fire.

spark, provides what is called activation energy. This energy provides just enough heat to turn some of the fuel into a gas, providing a sort of "jump start" to the burning process.

When something burns, the oxidation reaction can happen at many different speeds, depending on the kind of fuel that is used.

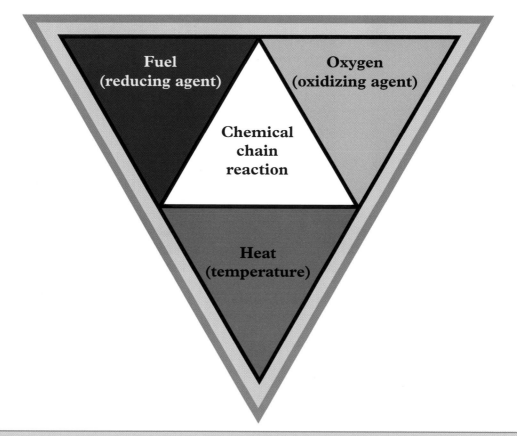

The fire triangle demonstrates the basic ingredients that make up fire. All of these things are necessary in order for a substance to ignite. The three main components are oxygen, heat, and fuel, such as firewood. Together, these three components will create a chemical reaction that will result in fire.

Oxidation is the same chemical process that turns iron into rust. But with iron, the reaction is very slow, and the heat energy that is released is very low. With certain things, like paper or wood, the oxidation rate of the molecules can be very fast. The heat is released in the form of flames.

Chapter Five
Oxygen Compounds

Elements chemically combine to form compounds, or combinations of elements. In chemistry, a compound is a substance formed from two or more elements. For example, water is a compound made out of two hydrogen atoms and one oxygen atom. Every compound has a chemical formula. This formula describes the number and kind of atoms in a substance. For example, in water, there are two hydrogen atoms for every one oxygen atom; therefore, it has a chemical formula of H_2O.

As we have already discussed, oxygen is one of the most reactive elements, meaning it combines easily with other elements. Rarely found alone in nature, it readily combines with almost every element, with the exception of helium (He), neon (Ne), argon (Ar), krypton (Kr), xenon (Xe), and radon (Rn). If you look at the periodic table, you'll see that most of these elements are within group 0 (or 18), and they are called inert gases. The word "inert" means that they are not active. These gases are called inert because they rarely react with anything at all.

Oxides

Compounds of oxygen and one other element are called oxides. As Antoine Lavoisier realized, oxides are often made by heating or burning an element or a compound in the presence of air or oxygen.

He

Ne

Ar

Kr

Xe

Rn

Uuo

The inert gases, formerly known as noble gases, are in group 0 (or 18) on the far right of the periodic table. While oxygen readily bonds with nearly every other element, it does not bond with the inert gases. Each element in this group has a full outer shell of electrons. Therefore, they are not ready to bond—even with oxygen.

Metal Oxides

When metals combine with oxygen, they form metal oxides, usually in the form of solid crystals. Magnesium oxide, for example, is actually white crystals, often mixed with magnesium chloride to form stucco, a light-colored cement often used to decorate the exterior of buildings.

Metal oxides are usually ionic compounds. Ionic compounds occur through the process of ionic bonding, in which the atoms of one element donate negatively charged electrons in their outer shells to the atoms of another element. In doing so, they become positively charged ions. In the case of metal oxides, the metal atoms donate electrons to oxygen atoms. The metal atom combines with an oxygen atom to form a compound. The metal atoms have become positively charged ions, while the oxygen atoms have become

Oxygen can be separated from compounds when an oxidizer is added. An oxidizer creates combustion, or the release of oxygen. Here, a test tube that contains hydrogen peroxide (H_2O_2) has the oxidizer manganese dioxide (MnO_2) added to it (photo 1). The reaction causes the hydrogen peroxide to bubble and break apart into water (H_2O) and oxygen (O_2). The bubbles are the oxygen.

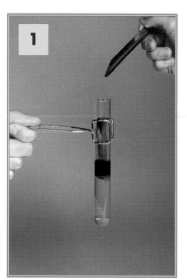

negatively charged ions. The opposite electrical charges cause the elements to bond together.

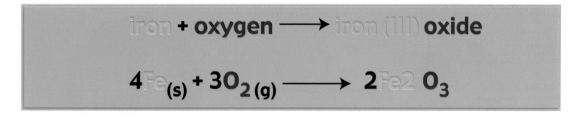

$$\text{iron} + \text{oxygen} \longrightarrow \text{iron (III) oxide}$$

$$4\,Fe_{(s)} + 3O_{2\,(g)} \longrightarrow 2\,Fe_2O_3$$

Nonmetal Oxides

Nonmetals combine differently with oxygen, choosing to share electrons rather than donating them to create nonmetal oxides. This process of sharing electrons is called covalent bonding, and this type of bond creates a molecule. Nonmetal oxides are usually very reactive and tend to form strong acids when dissolved in water. Their reactions are probably what Lavoisier observed when he coined the term "oxygen," or "acid former."

Oxidation and Reduction

Oxygen is involved in two important processes: oxidation and reduction. These processes are used in many everyday activities, from burning fuels to helping animals breathe, grow, and move. Originally, scientists used the term "oxidation" to mean that a substance was gaining oxygen. The term "reduction" meant that a substance was losing oxygen. Today, scientists use the terms oxidation and reduction to describe any reaction that involves the transfer of electrons. Atoms that lose electrons are said to be oxidized, and atoms that gain electrons are said to be reduced, even when oxygen is not involved. Any substance or compound that donates oxygen or accepts electrons to cause oxidation of another compound is called an oxidizing agent. Any substance that donates electrons to cause reduction is called a reducing agent.

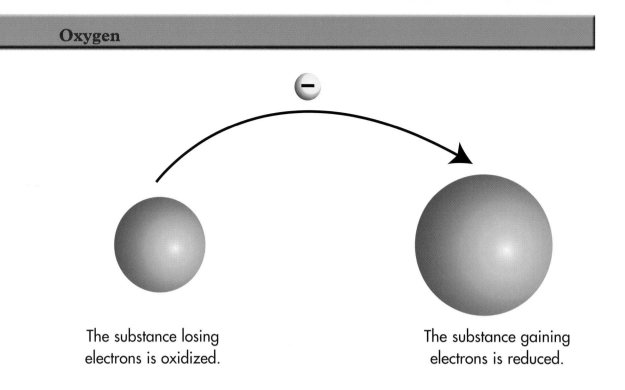

The substance losing electrons is oxidized.

The substance gaining electrons is reduced.

This model demonstrates the oxidation-reduction reaction between oxygen and another element. In this reaction, an element is oxidized when it loses one or more electrons. An element is reduced when it gains one or more electrons. Rust is one result of a common oxidation-reduction reaction. This is also called corrosion.

Rust

Rusting, for example, is an oxidation process. When exposed to air, most metals oxidize, forming a dull metal oxide coating or tarnish. In the case of aluminum (Al) or silver (Ag), this coating actually protects the untarnished metal below it from the air and further corrosion. However, when iron and steel are exposed to oxygen, a layer of brown iron oxide forms on the surface of the metal. This layer does not protect the metal below it from air and moisture. The metal merely crumbles away, and the rust can quickly "eat" through the metal. The only way to protect against this process is by applying a protective coating that seals the metal from air and moisture.

Oxidation is a key part of a Breathalyzer, a device that is used to help protect roadways from dangerous drunk drivers. A Breathalyzer works by oxidizing the alcohol in a person's breath. The more alcohol that is oxidized, the greater the electric current produced. This current sets off meters in the Breathalyzer. From these, law enforcement officials can judge how intoxicated a person is.

The Breathalyzer

The Breathalyzer test that police use to help protect people from drunk drivers also involves oxidation. By blowing into a tube, if the driver has been drinking, he or she blows into a tube on the Breathalyzer, where the alcohol on his or her breath is oxidized into a substance called ethanoic acid (acetic acid, or vinegar). This triggers an electric current. The strength of this current varies with the amount of ethanoic acid produced, which in turn varies with the amount a person has drunk. This is how police officers can tell when someone has had too much alcohol to drive safely.

Chapter Six
Oxygen and Life

Oxygen is involved in nearly every life process, including breathing, moving, and the digestion of food. Here, too, the process of combustion plays an important role—it provides energy to your body. Scientists have coined a special term for this "slow burn" process. It is called cellular respiration.

During digestion, nutrients within food are turned into a chemical called glucose and are carried to cells throughout the body. Glucose is a type of sugar. With help from oxygen, the glucose is burned within the cell and provides energy to help the body move and digest food, as well as carry out other important life functions. During this process, the hydrogen within the glucose combines with the oxygen to make water, which is absorbed by your body. Glucose also contains carbon, which combines with oxygen to create carbon dioxide, which cannot be used by the body. The carbon dioxide is removed from the body when you exhale, or breathe out.

When you breathe in, or inhale, you take oxygen from the air into your lungs. Each lung is lined with thousands of tiny passages, which are themselves covered with even tinier blood vessels. Oxygen from the air is breathed in and seeps through the walls of these blood vessels into the blood, where red blood cells transport the oxygen to all parts of your body. Oxygen is essential to all living tissue because it plays a

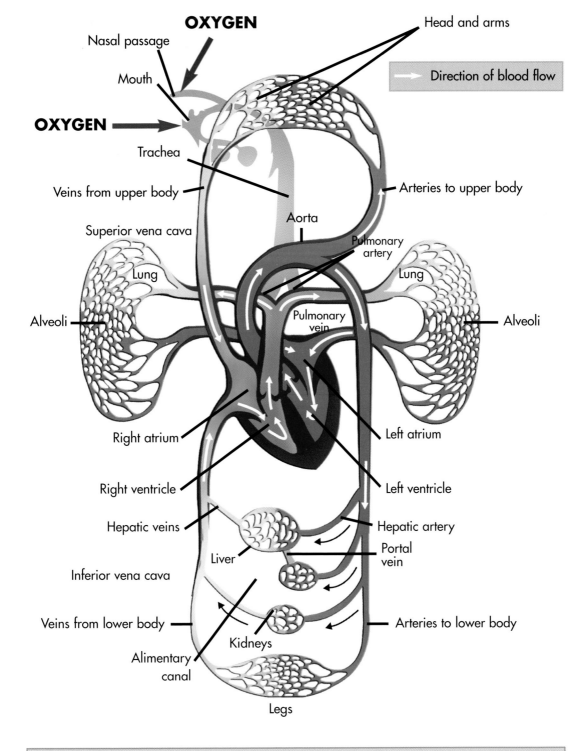

OXYGEN

Nasal passage

Mouth

OXYGEN

Trachea

Veins from upper body

Head and arms

Direction of blood flow

Aorta

Arteries to upper body

Superior vena cava

Pulmonary artery

Lung

Lung

Alveoli

Pulmonary vein

Alveoli

Right atrium

Left atrium

Right ventricle

Left ventricle

Hepatic veins

Hepatic artery

Liver

Portal vein

Inferior vena cava

Veins from lower body

Arteries to lower body

Kidneys

Alimentary canal

Legs

Oxygen plays an important role in your body's cardiovascular system *(above)*. The main function of the cardiovascular system is to deliver blood to and from the rest of the body. The heart acts as a pump, which moves the blood throughout the body. Oxygen is taken in through the lungs. The oxygen is then transferred to red blood cells through the alveoli, located in the lungs. The blood then flows through all the major arteries of the body where it dispenses the oxygen. The blood returns to the heart through the veins, and the cycle begins again.

role in the chemical processes important to life, including movement, eating, and reproduction. A special substance called hemoglobin helps deliver the essential gas to living tissue. It also helps carry the oxygen back to your lungs, where it can be exhaled as carbon dioxide.

The Oxygen Cycle

Inhaling oxygen and exhaling carbon dioxide are actually part of a larger process called the oxygen cycle. The oxygen cycle involves a constant exchange of air and oxygen between animals and plants. Animals, including humans, inhale oxygen from the air and exhale carbon dioxide. Plants absorb the carbon dioxide and release oxygen into the air through photosynthesis. Photosynthesis is the process by which green plants create food. Without plants, we wouldn't be able to breathe. Without us breathing, plants wouldn't be able to produce oxygen. And without oxygen, there would be no life on Earth.

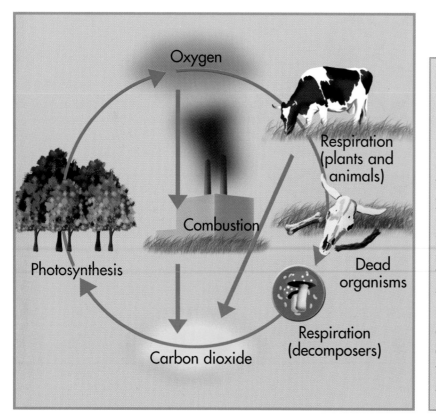

Every minute of every day, you are experiencing the oxygen cycle, also known as the carbon-oxygen cycle. The cycle begins with trees and green plants, which produce oxygen that is released into the air. Animals, such as humans, breathe in the oxygen to use as energy. Carbon dioxide is then exhaled. The carbon dioxide is used by the trees and plants as food.

Oxygen at Work

Although oxygen occurs naturally, it is often produced for use in many industries. These forms of oxygen can be found all around you.

Oxygen in a Bottle

After oxygen's discovery, one of the gas's earliest uses was in medicine. Hospitals still use bottled oxygen to help patients whose bodies are not strong enough to take it from the air. Patients are given pure oxygen, which goes right into their bloodstreams and helps them get healthy. Firefighters also use bottled oxygen in situations where the air is too dangerous to breathe normally. By carrying an oxygen tank and gas mask, firefighters are able to breathe inside a fire scene. Here, most of the oxygen is being used to fuel the fire. There is little oxygen left over, so breathing can be very difficult. Bottled oxygen is also used by climbers who travel to the highest mountain peaks, where the air is thin and oxygen is scarce. Divers also carry oxygen tanks to help them stay underwater for long periods of time.

Oxygen and Steel

Oxygen is also used to create steel. Workers use a blast of oxygen to remove dirt from molten steel before other metals are added to create the finished steel product. The world's steel industry is by far the largest user of commercially produced oxygen. However, many kinds of welding and cutting tools use oxygen to create the superhot temperatures often necessary to cut and mold iron, steel, and other hard metals.

It's easy to take oxygen for granted because it is truly everywhere on Earth. It plays a vital role in medicine and industry, and it is the one thing that you absolutely, positively cannot do without, even for a minute. In the end, oxygen really is the elixir of life in our world.

The Periodic Table of Elements

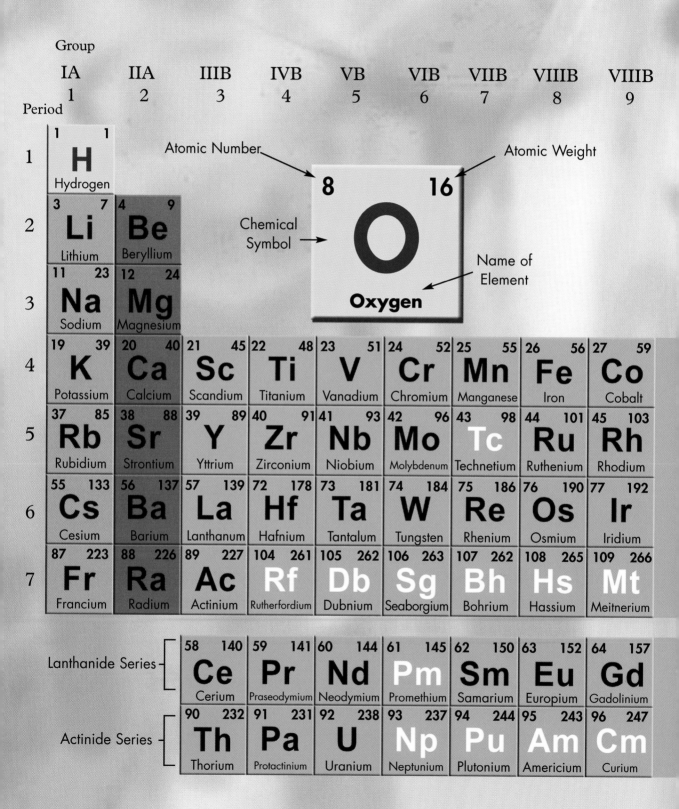

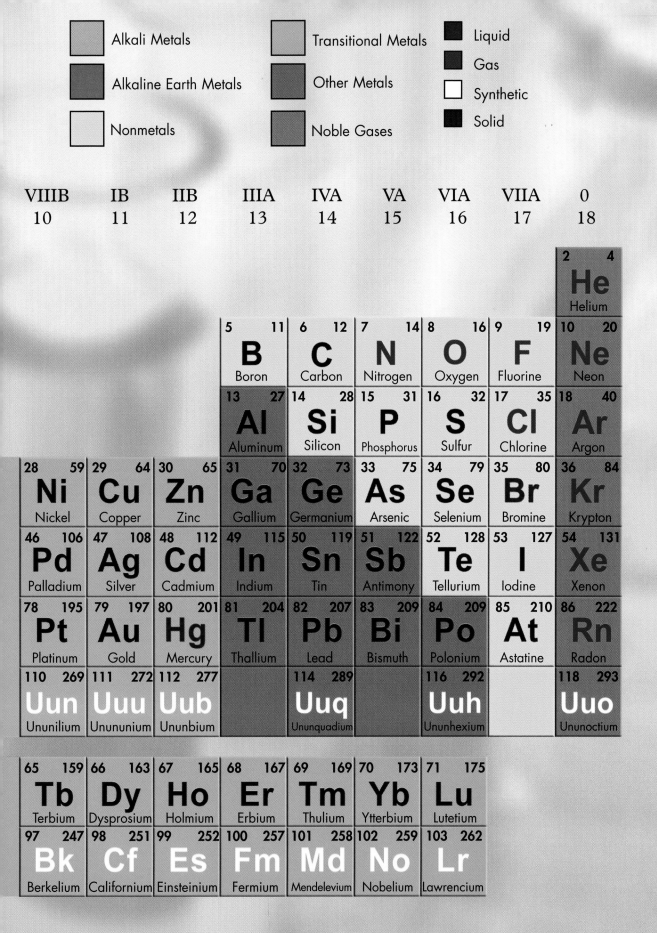

Glossary

alchemist A medieval scientist who tried to turn ordinary metals into precious metals and also sought to prolong life.

atmosphere The layer of gases around an object in space. On Earth, this layer is air.

atomic number The number of protons that exist within the nucleus of an atom. The atomic number determines an element's place on the periodic table.

combustion The process of combining with oxygen to burn.

distill To purify a liquid substance by condensation or evaporation.

electron A negatively charged particle found within an atom but outside of the nucleus.

isotope An atom of a chemical element with the same atomic number and nearly identical chemical behavior but with a different atomic weight and different physical properties.

molecule Two or more atoms bonded together.

neutron An atomic particle that has no electrical charge and is found inside the nucleus.

nucleus The center of an atom that contains protons and neutrons.

oxidation The process by which oxygen is added to something or by which atoms donate electrons.

photosynthesis The process in which green plants make their own food from sunlight, water, and carbon dioxide.

proton A subatomic particle that has a positive electrical charge and is found inside the nucleus.

reduction The process by which oxygen is removed from something or by which atoms gain electrons.

For More Information

American Chemical Society
1155 Sixteenth Street NW
Washington, DC 20036
Web site: http://www.acs.org/education

National Aeronautics and Space Administration (NASA)
Office of Education/NASA Headquarters
Washington, DC 20546
Web site: http://kids.msfc.nasa.gov

National Geographic Society
1145 Seventeenth Street NW
Washington, DC 20036
Web site: http://www.nationalgeographic.com/kids

The Smithsonian Institution
Smithsonian Center for Education and Museum Studies
P.O. Box 37012/A&I 1163, MRC 402
Washington, DC 20013
Web site: http://www.smithsonian.kids.us

Web Sites

Due to the changing nature of Internet links, the Rosen Publishing Group, Inc., has developed an online list of Web sites related to the subject of this book. This site is updated regularly. Please use this link to access the list:

http://www.rosenlinks.com/uept/oxyg

45

For Further Reading

Atkins, P. W. *The Periodic Kingdom*. New York: Basic Books, 1997.

Karukstis, Kerry K., and Gerald Van Hecke. *Chemistry Connections: The Chemical Basis of Everyday Phenomena*. New York: Academic Press, 2003.

Newmark, Ann. *Chemistry*. New York: DK Publishing, 1999.

Oxlade, Chris. *Elements & Compounds* (Chemicals in Action). Portsmouth, NH: Heinemann Library, 2002.

Bibliography

Emsley, John. *Molecules at an Exhibition: Portraits of Intriguing Materials in Everyday Life*. New York: Oxford University Press, 1998.

Elmsley, John. *Nature's Building Blocks: An A–Z Guide to the Elements*. New York: Oxford University Press, 2003.

Heiserman, David L. *Exploring Chemical Elements and Their Compounds*. New York: McGraw-Hill Trade, 1991.

Lane, Nick. *Oxygen: The Molecule That Made the World*. New York: Oxford University Press, 2002.

LeMay, H. Eugene, Jr. *Chemistry: Connections to Our Changing World*. Englewood Cliffs, NJ: Prentice Hall, 2000.

Stwertka, Albert. *A Guide to the Elements*. New York: Oxford University Press Children's Books, 1999.

About the Author

Journalist and freelance editor Michele Thomas has covered health and nutrition for *Muscle Media* magazine and was the managing editor of Metro Newspaper Service. She has also worked on science programs for Newbridge Educational Publishing and Macmillan/McGraw-Hill. She lives in her native Brooklyn, New York, with Stitches the cat.

Photo Credits

Cover, pp. 1, 9, 10, 12, 16, 17, 21, 22, 32, 36, 39, 40 by Tahara Hasan; pp. 5, 18 courtesy of NASA; p. 7 © Bettmann/Corbis ; p. 15 © Library of Congress, Prints and Photographs Division; p. 24 © Corbis; p. 26 © Images.com/Corbis; p. 27 © Health and Safety Laboratory/Photo Researchers, Inc.; p. 28 © Jean-Louis Charnet/ Photo Researchers, Inc.; pp. 31, 34 by Maura McConnell; p. 37 © Jim Varney/Photo Researchers, Inc.

Special thanks to Rosemarie Alken and Westtown School, in Westtown, Pennsylvania.

Designer: Tahara Hasan; Editor: Charles Hofer